# My F‹

MW00713999

Adria F. Klein

Illustrated by David Preston Smith

## DOMINIE PRESS
Pearson Learning Group

I have a mother.

I have a mother and a father.

I have a mother and a father
and a big brother.

I have a mother and a father
and a big brother and a
little sister.

I have a mother and a father
and a big brother and a little
sister and a dog named Rusty.

I have a mother and a father
and a big brother and a little
sister and a dog named Rusty
and a cat named Fluffy.

I have a great family.